Published by Ice House Books

Copyright © 2019 Ice House Books

Written by Moira Butterfield
Illustrated by Pedro Demetriou
Designed by Emily Curtis

Ice House Books is an imprint of Half Moon Bay Limited
The Ice House, 124 Walcot Street, Bath, BA1 5BG
www.icehousebooks.co.uk

ISBN 978-1-912867-10-3

Printed in China

WHEN THERE'S A ZOMBIE IN YOUR KITCHEN...

ICE HOUSE BOOKS

WHEN THE ZOMBIES ARE COMING

WHAT IF THINGS TURN BAD AND A ZOMBIE APOCALYPSE BEGINS?

AND HERE IS THE NEWS, ZOMBIES ARE... AAAAAAARGH!

NEWS TV

NO WORRIES!

Well, some worries, obviously, but this book should help you survive an undead invasion. First, you need to be able to recognise a zombie and stop it before it takes a bite.

LOOK CAREFULLY AT THE PERSON COMING TOWARDS YOU AND TICK THESE BOXES FAST. IF YOU GET TO THE LAST ONE, RUN!

THIS COULD JUST BE A DRUNK PERSON, SO DELAY DECAPITATING THEM FOR A MOMENT...

1. They stagger along.

2. Their outfit is torn and tattered.

3. They moan instead of speaking.

4. They are covered in open wounds.

5. They stink like the slimiest piece of out-of-date meat you ever found in the fridge.

6. They are chewing on a body part.

YUP, THAT'S ENOUGH TICKS. GET THE HELL OUTTA THERE!

WHEN YOU WANT TO ZOMBIE-PROOF YOUR HOUSE

THE UNDEAD ARE A DIY NIGHTMARE.

They're really clumsy and they will crash through glass and doors, leaving an unsightly mess as well as attacking everyone they find inside. Stop them getting in to make a meal of you and your interiors by blocking up your doors and windows with planks and nails.

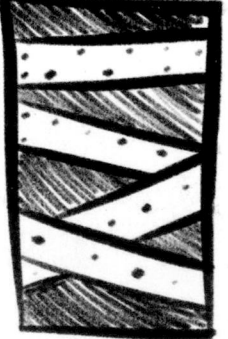

An attic is a good hide-out option because zombies are usually too clumsy to climb ladders, and if they do make it to the top you can hit them over the head with some attic rubbish you forgot you owned.

Remember to nail up letter flaps and cat flaps if you don't want to get grabbed by a grisly hand unexpectedly poking through.

WHEN YOU GET INTO A ZOMBIE FIGHT

WHAT IF YOU FIND YOURSELF FACE-TO-ROTTING-FACE WITH A ZOMBIE?

Zombies don't feel pain, so it's no good kicking them where it hurts (those bits may have fallen off, anyway).

They don't get tired, either, so you really have only one option in a fight – **FINISH THEM OFF.**

YOU CAN DO THIS IN TWO WAYS:

1. Squish the head with a heavy weapon.

2. Cut it off with a handy sharp implement.

You'll just be making
yourself into a
convenient picnic.

DON'T curl up and play
dead, hoping the zombie will
lurch on by. It's brainless, and
soon you will be, too.

A ZOMBIE'S HEAD IS LIKE A
GHERKIN IN A BURGER BUN.
IT'S SMELLY AND POINTLESS.

NOTHING GOES ON IN THERE
SO DON'T FEEL BAD ABOUT
BASHING IT, BOILED-EGG STYLE.

WHEN A ZOMBIE
IS CHASING YOU

Remember that zombies are slow, clumsy and stupid, so you will have a big advantage in a chase. If you meet a fast, clever one, it's probably somebody in fancy dress.*

NO NEED TO PANIC. THE ZOMBIE DUDE BEHIND YOU CAN'T RUN FOR TOFFEE. IT'S THE DUDES IN FRONT YOU HAVE TO WORRY ABOUT.

DON'T FORGET TO LOOK AHEAD, OR YOU MIGHT LOSE YOUR HEAD.

*Please note, however. We take no responsibility for zombie mutations. It's your call.

DON'T FORGET TO LOOK AHEAD OF YOU as you run. If there's a zombie horde they'll be coming from all sides. You're better off getting into a car at this point and driving towards your enemy. Zombies bounce really well.

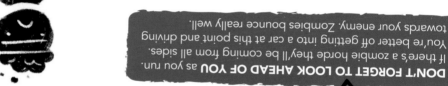

- RUN FAST. BETTER STILL, GET ON A BICYCLE. ZOMBIES DON'T PEDAL WELL DUE TO THEIR FEET FALLING OFF. THEY'RE QUITE GOOD AT HOLDING THE HANDLEBARS, THOUGH.

- ZIG ZAG AS YOU RUN. ZOMBIES TEND TO LURCH IN STRAIGHT LINES.

WHEN YOU HAVE TO CLEAN UP AFTER A
ZOMBIE ATTACK

HAVE YOU BEEN LEFT WITH A DISTRESSING MESS OF STAINS
AND GOOEY LUMPS IN YOUR HOME?

Don't get downhearted. Get to work with
stain removers and think about upcycling
some of the zombie limbs left behind.

Blood spray on the patio?
Soak it in cola overnight.

LAMP

REMOTE-CONTROL HOLDER

ZOMBIE
UPCYCLING
IDEAS

Bloodstains on clothing or furniture? Cover with a paste of talcum powder mixed with water and allow to dry before wiping away.

Check with your local recycling service for the best way to dispose of large amounts of zombie parts. You may have to pay an excess gore supplement.

WHEN YOUR BARISTA IS A ZOMBIE

WHEN ZOMBIES START TURNING UP IN YOUR COFFEE SHOP AND OTHER EVERYDAY PLACES, YOU'LL NEED TO KNOW THESE SPECIAL FIGHT MOVES.

ZOMBIE ALERT: BARISTA
Order a cup of decaf soy latte, extra hot, no foam, and then throw it into their rotting beardy face. It will taste like a cup of pretentious piddle anyway, and it will give you time to run.

ZOMBIE ALERT: SHOP ASSISTANT
Swing a wire basket into the face of the mouldering shop cashier and follow up by throwing heavy weapons such as tins of tomatoes. By the time you've finished, the 'unexpected item in bagging area' will be a zombie body part.

ZOMBIE ALERT: DENTIST
Throw the mouthwash, then grab the drill and deal with the dentist, but watch out for the dental receptionist sneaking up on you from behind. Receptionists of all kinds can be as mean as snakes, with or without zombie brains.

ZOMBIE ALERT: HAIRDRESSER
Use a brush or hairdryer to distract the zombie with one hand and grab the scissors with the other hand, to give your horrific hairdresser their own final cut and dye.

WHEN YOU SIT BY A ZOMBIE IN THE CINEMA

IT'S DARK AND THE MOVIE'S ABOUT TO BEGIN WHEN A STRANGE MAN SLIPS INTO THE EMPTY SEAT NEXT TO YOU.

Does he seem normal or is he a zombie film-goer? You can't be sure. The rotten side of his face might be on the side you can't see, so be alert for these undead giveaway signs:

He's crunching on something but it's not popcorn. It sounds more bony....

That's not the smell of aftershave. It's the smell of afterdeath.

He reminds you of someone you once saw in a movie. Who is it now? Matt Damon? Tom Cruise? No, wait. **It's a ZOMBIE.**

He's not sucking noisily on a milkshake straw. He's sucking noisily on the brains of the guy in front (zombies have no eating manners).

He's not biting his nails… he's biting yours.

Get out of the cinema fast if you want a happy ending. Leave the movie to the monster. It's probably rotten, like him, anyway.

WHEN YOU THINK YOUR NEXT-DOOR NEIGHBOUR IS A ZOMBIE

DO YOU SUSPECT YOUR ACTUAL NEXT-DOOR NEIGHBOUR IS A ZOMBIE? YOU CAN'T AFFORD TO LET IT SLIDE BECAUSE, NEXT THING YOU KNOW, HE'LL BE COMING INTO YOUR HOUSE UNINVITED TO BORROW A PLATE OF YOUR TASTY BRAINS.

Does he work at night – what they call **THE GRAVEYARD SHIFT?**

Does he drive an old **BONESHAKER** of a car that looks like it came from the scrapheap? The perfect model for a zombie, right? Do bits fall off it, just like him?

Does his garden design remind you of a cemetery, with rows of headstones instead of rows of beans in the veg patch?

Does someone else in the street disappear every time he has a barbecue?

Are his kids always kicking their football over the fence into your plot? And if that's a football, why does it have ears and look like the guy from number 7?

When your neighbours are zombies **YOU'VE GOT TO GET TOUGH.** Get out the hedge trimmer with the extra-sharp blades....
You know what you have to do, and it isn't a spot of gardening.

WHEN A ZOMBIE IS IN YOUR KITCHEN

LET'S SAY THAT YOU FAILED TO SOLVE THE PROBLEM OF YOUR ZOMBIE NEIGHBOURS.

Now one of them is in your kitchen. Who are you gonna call? Nobody. It's down to you, and you'd better be quick before you find yourself **ON THE SPECIALS MENU.**

Stuff your zombie neighbour's hand in the blender, switch it to **MAX** and then make your escape, trying not to think about the smoothie you just made.

*Don't know of one in your area? Why not ask your local homeware store manager to provide more zombie-aware products in-store?

Use your kitchen knives. We recommend that home chefs buy a dual-purpose zombie/fish-filleting set from a zombie-aware home supplier.*

Do you have a chest freezer? Trip up your zombie neighbour and shut them inside. Zombies are incredibly strong and he/she will eventually punch their way out, but you'll have time to leave.**

**Never eat from this freezer again, especially not joints of meat.

WHEN A ZOMBIE IS IN YOUR KITCHEN

So if you know of a zombie outbreak in your locality, why not keep a few brain-like foods in the fridge to waylay them? That could give you the breathing space you need to grab a knife and start displaying your chopping skills on the greedy ghoul.

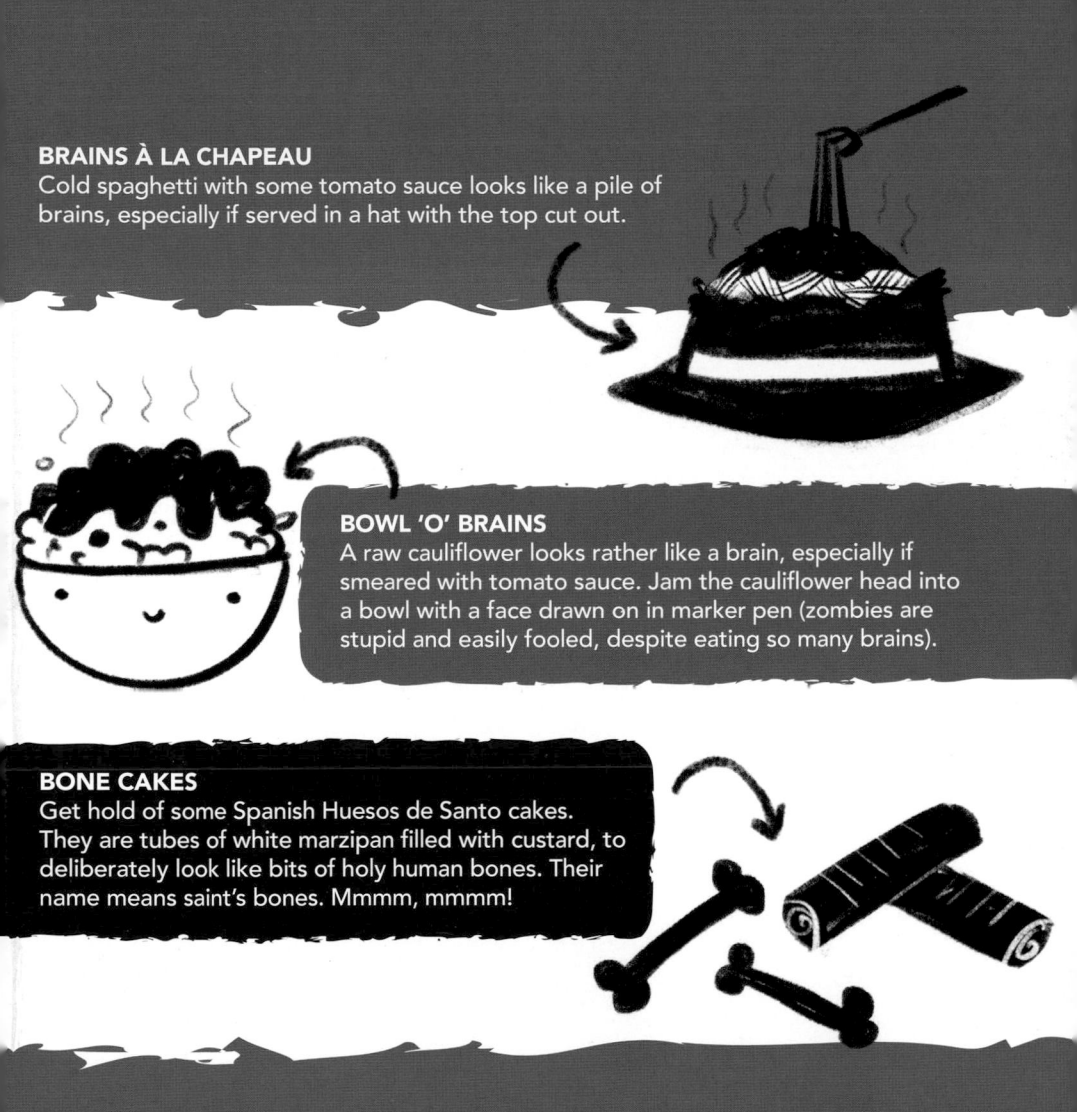

BRAINS À LA CHAPEAU
Cold spaghetti with some tomato sauce looks like a pile of brains, especially if served in a hat with the top cut out.

BOWL 'O' BRAINS
A raw cauliflower looks rather like a brain, especially if smeared with tomato sauce. Jam the cauliflower head into a bowl with a face drawn on in marker pen (zombies are stupid and easily fooled, despite eating so many brains).

BONE CAKES
Get hold of some Spanish Huesos de Santo cakes. They are tubes of white marzipan filled with custard, to deliberately look like bits of holy human bones. Their name means saint's bones. Mmmm, mmmm!

WHEN YOU WANT TO TRAP A ZOMBIE

DO YOU FIND THE WHOLE HEAD-CUTTING-OFF THING A BIT TOO GRUESOME?

If you're that way inclined, you may feel you want to humanely trap your undead corpse colleagues. Are you crazy? It's a terrible idea, worse than a vegan getting a job in a sausage factory. It's not going to end well.

Oh, ok. If you really must, it can be done, but zombie-baiting is a specialist job and we recommend that you practise the method shown below on willing friends before trying it for real*.

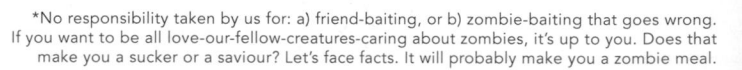

*No responsibility taken by us for: a) friend-baiting, or b) zombie-baiting that goes wrong. If you want to be all love-our-fellow-creatures-caring about zombies, it's up to you. Does that make you a sucker or a saviour? Let's face facts. It will probably make you a zombie meal.

1. Dig a pit deep enough to stop a zombie climbing out.

2. Bait the pit with tinned processed meat, which is quite close in taste to disgusting human remains. This should attract a zombie.

3. When a zombie falls into the pit, keep it there and phone your local zombie collection service**.

**If you find there is no zombie collection service, take that as a lesson to think things through properly before you do your let's-save-the-ghouls act. Anyway, what do you think a zombie collection service would do with your zombie friend? One word. Landfill.

WHEN YOUR PARTNER IS A ZOMBIE

WHAT IF YOUR BELOVED GETS BITTEN AND BECOMES A ZOMBIE?

Let's be honest. It's not ideal because they won't be their old self – more of a green decaying version. But it's understandable if you want to keep them as safe and secure as you can.

You'll have to put heavy chains on your beloved to stop them escaping, but there's no reason why you can't keep them in a convenient outbuilding. You could even install a TV so they can watch zombie movies, which are like documentaries for them.

We strongly advise installing air con, if you want your zombie to last longer in hot weather.

BEWARE! GUARD ZOMBIE

YOUR ZOMBIE PARTNER CAN STILL BE USEFUL BECAUSE THEY MAKE A GREAT SUBSTITUTE FOR A GUARD DOG.

You can't feed your zombie human flesh, obvs, but try treats such as **faggots** (meat balls made with animal offal), **pork scratchings** (which look quite like human ears), and **cheap sausages** (because nobody has any idea what's in those).

WHEN YOUR PARTNER IS A ZOMBIE

Your zombie has no meaningful thoughts.
You could enter it as a contestant in a reality TV show.

Enjoy dancing with your zombie (not too near).
They already know the moves to Thriller.

Take your zombie out at Halloween.
They will blend in, and when you want to do trick or treat, they make an awesome trick.

Share a hot tub. Bits fall off, OK? 'Nuff said.

Don't expect your zombie to be tidy around the home. They're going to leave more than just dirty socks lying around.

Organise a date night.
The whole idea stinks, and so will your date.

WHEN YOU WANT TO STYLE A ZOMBIE

IS YOUR ZOMBIE PARTNER OR FRIEND LETTING THEMSELVES GO? IT'S SADLY INEVITABLE. COULD YOU HELP WITH THE OFFER OF A STYLING MAKEOVER?

GOOD ZOMBIE LOOKS
A full mummy wrap holds the figure together, literally, and hides unsightly areas (ie: everything).

Direct eyes away from problem areas with the use of accessories such as gold chains (securely locked).

ZOMBIE MAKE-UP
This is a tough one. Even the heaviest make-up will struggle to even out zombie skin tones. Wall plaster is the only brand recommended.

ZOMBIE FASHION NO-NOs
Tight body-con outfits or lycra cycling gear. These are unforgiving on the figure and all too obviously reveal body faults (such as missing parts).

WHEN YOU WANT TO MAKE A ZOMBIE LAUGH

TRY THESE JOKES TO CHEER A ZOMBIE UP AND SEE THEM LAUGH THEIR HEAD OFF.

Do zombies eat popcorn with their fingers?
No. They eat the fingers separately.

Why did the zombie lose a case in court?
He didn't have a leg to stand on.

What's a zombie's favourite dessert?
Is it I-scream?

WHEN YOUR WORK COLLEAGUES ARE ZOMBIES

YOU'LL NEED SOME LIFE HACKS FAST IF YOU COME INTO WORK TO FIND YOUR WORKPLACE ZOMBIFIED.

Let's just check you're not imagining this. Some offices just seem like they are staffed by the undead.

Are your colleagues particularly moany?
Are they at each other's throats (literally)?
Has the population of office flies exploded?
Are there body parts instead of chocolate biscuits in the office kitchen?

If you're absolutely sure they've all gone zombie, you're going to have to wield the office chainsaw (usually kept somewhere in the boss's office in case cuts need to be made). To be on the safe side, send an internal email first.

WHEN CELEBRITIES ARE ZOMBIES

GET THE KNACK OF SPOTTING ZOMBIES HIDING IN THE PUBLIC EYE.

Celebrities who have had a lot of plastic surgery are usually hiding the fact that their real body parts got left behind somewhere.

ZOMBIES!

Sporting zombie celebrities usually play football. They often attack other players and get a lot of red cards.

Why do actors look so convincing in zombie movies? Because it's so much cheaper to cast the real undead. You can pay them in offal.

Why can't you see the legs of many news presenters? Because they dropped off, that's why!

WHEN YOU MEET A ZOMBIE ON HOLIDAY

ZOMBIES ARE DIFFERENT AROUND THE WORLD. READ OUR GUIDE, SO AT LEAST YOU'LL KNOW ROUGHLY WHAT KIND OF CREATURE IS GROANING OUTSIDE YOUR HOTEL DOOR.

AFRICA & THE CARIBBEAN

The name 'zombie' is said to derive from an African word for a supernatural creature. It spread when people were captured as slaves from the region and sent to work in Haiti. There the idea developed that zombies could be created and controlled by powerful voodoo shamans casting spells, but they say you can send these unfortunate shaman-servant zombies back to the grave by giving them some salt.

NEW ORLEANS

It's rumoured you can be turned into a zombie and controlled by a voodoo shaman if you venture too far into the mysterious corners of New Orleans. So be careful which bar you go into and if you see a guy with a black top hat and cane, don't get too friendly. That's a shaman look.

SOUTHERN EUROPE

The Ancient Greeks wrote of re-animating the dead, and in ancient Sicily graves were covered in heavy stones to make sure that the corpse didn't turn up again. It's probably best not to have a holiday picnic on the stones, just in case…

HOLLYWOOD

Zombies of all kinds have been created in Hollywood movies, and some of them can run fast, which is very bad news. An invasion of those super-bad-boy zombies would mean that no holiday destination was safe, and it would probably be necessary to live at sea or on a space station, maybe.

HAPPY HOLIDAYS!

WHEN EVERYONE IS A ZOMBIE BUT YOU

IF YOU FIND THAT YOU'RE THE LAST HUMAN LEFT STANDING YOU'LL HAVE TO PRETEND THAT YOU'RE A ZOMBIE, TOO, TO SURVIVE.

THE WALK
Make your arms and legs stiff. No bending. Walk as if you've been covered in cement.

UUURRGGGGHHH …

THE TALK
Groan and moan in a low tone. Say nothing, even if you stub your toe and really, really want to say bad words (zombies don't feel pain).

REMEMBER

Zombies don't jog – so walk slowly.

Zombies don't scratch itches – they don't feel anything.

Zombies don't sneeze – though you can get away with farting.

Zombies don't go to the toilet – you'll have to pee in secret.

Zombies don't giggle – think of something horrible, like zombies, to stop yourself getting a giggling fit.

Zombies don't sleep – don't nod off and start snoring. If you do, you're doomed.

WHEN EVERYONE IS A ZOMBIE BUT YOU

YOU'LL NEED A ZOMBIE DISGUISE, USING ANY MAKE-UP YOU HAVE HANDY OR ITEMS FROM AROUND THE HOUSE.

HAIR – Very, very messy. Not so much bedhead as deadhead.

DEAD-LOOKING SKIN – Pale make-up foundation or flour dusted on.

SCABBY BITS – Flour and water paste mixed with green or red food colouring, dabbed onto the skin to dry.

DARK EYE CIRCLES – Black eye pencil or charcoal rubbed in with your finger.

BLOOD-BASED EATING HABITS – Tomato sauce dribbles from the sides of the mouth.

SMELL – Carry around some rotten pieces of fish or get yourself sprayed by a handy skunk.

WHEN YOU'RE TEMPTED BY ZOMBIE
LIFE

THE HORDES ARE AT YOUR DOOR. ARE YOU THINKING OF GIVING UP THE FIGHT AND GOING FULL ZOMBIE? WEIGH UP THE PROS AND CONS.

WHY REJECT ZOMBIE LIFE?
It could turn your head. Right round backwards.

Your career, love life and skin will suffer while you spend all your time looking for brains to eat.

Zombies are dead boring. They follow the crowd.

WHY GIVE UP?
You won't have to worry about how you look or smell ever again.

You won't need to earn a living, because you'll be undead.

You won't have to pretend to like people. You can eat them instead.

Your shopping bills will go down.

WHEN YOU'RE TEMPTED BY ZOMBIE LIFE

HELP MAKE THAT DECISION ABOUT BECOMING A ZOMBIE BY TAKING THIS HANDY QUIZ. CHOOSE A, B OR C AND ADD UP YOUR CHOICES, THEN EITHER KEEP FIGHTING OR GO AND GET YOURSELF BITTEN.

AROUND THE HOUSE

- **A** You keep your room tidy. You hate mess.
- **B** You tidy up roughly once a week but not always.
- **C** Why tidy your room? It just gets messy again.

YOUR HAIR ROUTINE

- **A** You go to the hairdresser's regularly, roughly every 6 weeks.
- **B** You go to the hairdresser's occasionally, when you want to change your style.
- **C** You cut your own hair with kitchen scissors.

YOUR TIMEKEEPING

A You hate people being late.

B You are sometimes late because you forget to look at the time.

C Being late is normal. Don't sweat it. Get a life.

YOUR PERSONAL SCENT

A You always wear your favourite perfume or aftershave.

B You can't decide which perfume or aftershave you like best, and you often forget to put one on.

C You never wear perfume or aftershave because you think most of it smells like a chemical attack.

YOUR RESTAURANT HABITS

A You try to make healthy food choices in restaurants.

B You try to order healthily in restaurants but then you see the dessert menu and it all goes wrong.

C You order a burger if possible – a triple-cheeseburger, and there's no room for dessert.

MOSTLY A :

You are not cut out for zombie life because you are far too fastidious and fussy. The mess, the smell, the flesh-eating…it's so not you. Keep fighting.

MOSTLY B :

You are a ditherer, unable to decide things. The zombie life might suit you because you won't have to make any more choices, so it's probably best to get off the fence and become a fiend.

MOSTLY C :

You are already part-zombified so you may as well go the whole undead distance. Your friends might not even notice.

WHEN YOU GET BITTEN

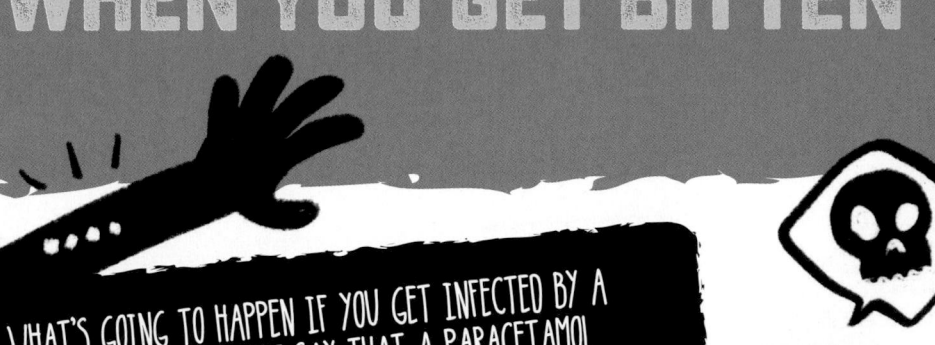

WHAT'S GOING TO HAPPEN IF YOU GET INFECTED BY A ZOMBIE BITE? LET'S JUST SAY THAT A PARACETAMOL AND A PLASTER ISN'T GOING TO CUT IT.

HOUR 1
You notice bruising and a painful wound. Have you had zombie contact? If not, relax. If you have, alert your friends and isolate yourself. You're going zombie!

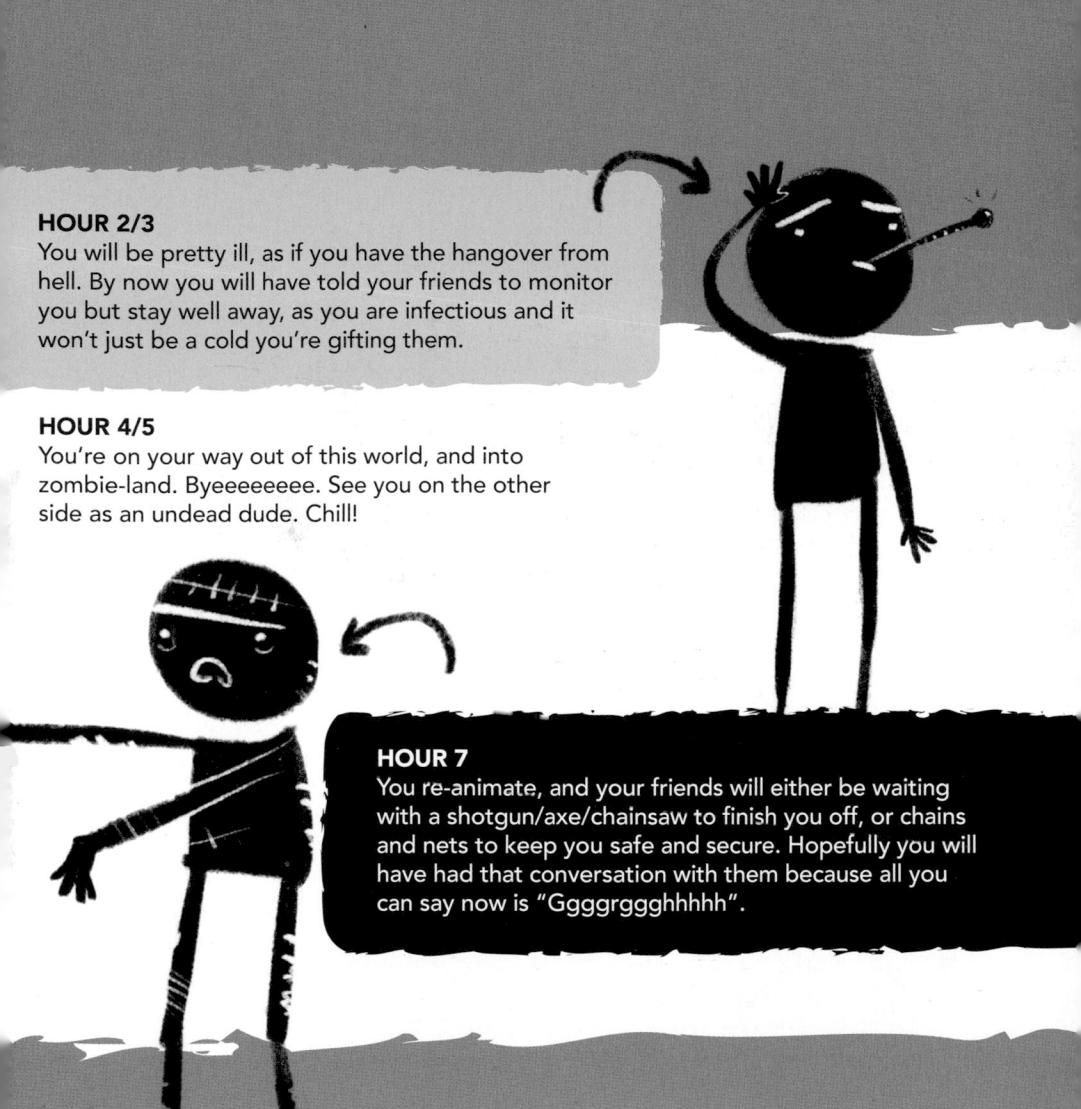

HOUR 2/3

You will be pretty ill, as if you have the hangover from hell. By now you will have told your friends to monitor you but stay well away, as you are infectious and it won't just be a cold you're gifting them.

HOUR 4/5

You're on your way out of this world, and into zombie-land. Byeeeeeeee. See you on the other side as an undead dude. Chill!

HOUR 7

You re-animate, and your friends will either be waiting with a shotgun/axe/chainsaw to finish you off, or chains and nets to keep you safe and secure. Hopefully you will have had that conversation with them because all you can say now is "Ggggrggghhhhh".

WHEN YOU GET BITTEN

IF YOU'RE ABOUT TO BE A ZOMBIE THERE ARE SOME CHANGES YOU CAN DO QUICKLY TO MAKE YOUR AFTERLIFE EASIER.

Start using dandruff shampoo now, and your head will disintegrate more slowly later on.
You know you're worth it.

Drink and eat as much as you want. Seven cocktails and a bottle of rum? Why not? A whole banoffi pie and a doughnut side? Go for it. There'll be no room for regret when you're re-animated.

Change your social media tags to @rottingzombie. That way friends will be prepared for your terrifying new selfies.

I ♥ U 4 UR BRAINS

Lay out a set of clothes you know you'll be comfortable in when you go on a lurching mass attack with a horde of your new zombie friends. Choose something well-made, so it will last an afterlife-time.

WHEN YOU NEED A ZOMBIE LIFE HACK

OK, SO YOU MAY BE A ZOMBIE, BUT LIKE EVERYONE ELSE YOU ARE GOING TO HAVE LIFE PROBLEMS : WELL, UNDEAD PROBLEMS, ANYWAY. HERE ARE SOME ANSWERS TO TYPICAL QUERIES RECEIVED FROM THE RECENTLY ZOMBIFIED.

My old friends don't want to mix with me now I've zombietrans'ed. It's not surprising. You have changed. They haven't. Move on and find a zombie horde where you can make new brain-chomping chums.

My love life is a disaster now I'm a zombie
Yes, this is a common problem because zombies have no feelings. Be prepared to get your heart broken...and also eaten. Don't expect a lasting zombie relationship because zombies can't hold it together for long. They're hard work because they're always falling apart.

My wife wants a divorce now I'm a zombie
Sorry. It's time to split up and let things drop, then pick up the pieces.

WHEN YOU NEED A
ZOMBIE LIFE HACK

HERE ARE SOME COMMON LIFE PROBLEMS THAT ARE ACTUALLY SOLVED BY BEING A ZOMBIE.

I can't keep my spending under control and I have spiralling debts.

The zombie answer: Smash your way into a bank. You'll find lots of money lying about in piles, along with the bank employees.

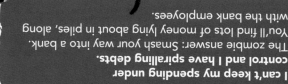

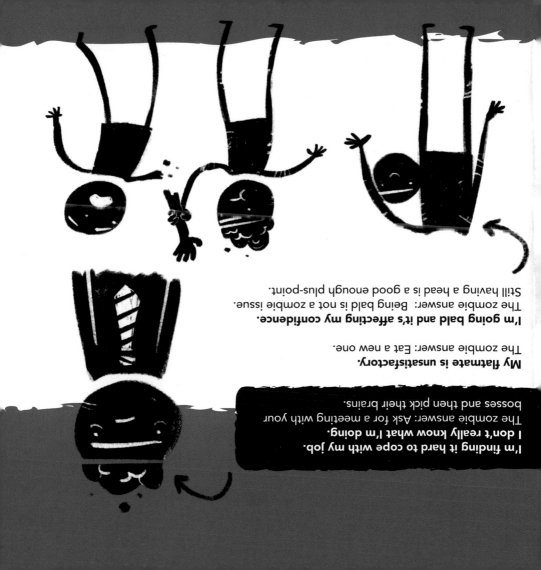

I'm finding it hard to cope with my job.
I don't really know what I'm doing.
The zombie answer: Ask for a meeting with your bosses and then pick their brains.

My flatmate is unsatisfactory.
The zombie answer: Eat a new one.

I'm going bald and it's affecting my confidence.
The zombie answer: Being bald is not a zombie issue. Still having a head is a good enough plus-point.

WHEN YOU'VE BECOME OVER-OBSESSED WITH ZOMBIES

IT'S UNDERSTANDABLE. YOU'VE JUST READ A WHOLE BOOK ABOUT THEM. IN FACT, PSYCHOLOGISTS SAY THAT ZOMBIES HAVE BECOME A POPULAR STRAND IN CULTURE BECAUSE:

1. We fear being controlled and manipulated ourselves in our modern highly-connected world.

2. We fear mass disasters in the modern world.

3. We identify with zombies because they represent our secret underlying rages.

STUFF ABOUT ZOMBIES

Or perhaps we're just like scary
stuff because it's kind of a laugh.

Your call, zombie fan. Is it
complicated or is it comedy?

2.

3.

WHEN YOU'VE BECOME OVER-OBSESSED WITH ZOMBIES

LOOK, YOU COULD JUST STOP READING ABOUT THEM, RIGHT HERE! IN FACT, IF YOU'RE REALLY GETTING OBSESSED, AND YOU CAN'T SLEEP AT NIGHT BECAUSE YOU THINK THEY MIGHT BE COMING, READ THIS SENTENCE OUT LOUD...

...THEY'RE NOT REAL, YOU IDIOT!

And anyway, zombies eat brains, so you're safe, right?

Wait a minute. There's someone coming through the front door.

Hey, they didn't even knock! That's so ru........